COUNCIL FLAT PARADISE

BY WILL ROGERS

- RUFF RUFF PUBLISHING - LONDON -

First Edition 1988.
Second Edition 1990.
Third Edition 1994.

ISBN: 0-9547078-0-X

Cover Design by Will Rogers.
Foreword pic by Claudette Atkinson.
All other pics by Chris Barton except map.
Designed in schmoo. Printed by GA Type.

CONTENTS

FOREWORD

F *oreword ever backward* never! Yes rude bwoy! This is the original Brixton Cockney Yardie telling you how to grow the best Ganja, and all in the environment of your council flat, to make you know seh. A nuh nutting, any bad bwoy can do it. Anyway hold tight rude bwoy, build up a bighead spliff and relax and settle cos we're going on a journey. A journey to agriculture. A journey from the seed to the root to the rizla.

So hold tight! Aaaal rude gal buckle up! Rude bwoy show dem seh you have the remedy!!'

(1) SEEDS. (BASICS)

Now listen here bad bwoy. A whole heap of people feel that the seeds you use are not very important, but this is a big mistake.

Yes, I know you can buy a bag of seeds from any fishing tackle and bait store, or you've pulled out the boombastic seeds from out of your *boom draw of yard sess*, but these are of an inferior stock due to them being imported seeds, probably from a hot climate and of a stock grown for its seed yield and not for the size of the bud.

The problem escalates when the seeds natural habitat is of a different hemisphere, of a different climate and of a different length growing season.

While these seeds will still grow and even bud they are far from the best seeds that you can use. Try to get seeds that are already acclimatised, in other words from the same Continent, and with the same length of growing season. As this is London we want European seeds (other seeds take upwards of three generations to acclimatise, or so I've heard.

Luckily we now have many European stocks of 'weed' to choose from (thanks to the Dutch), the most popular of these being the notorious 'Skunk' and 'Super Skunks' and the infamous 'Hazes'.

These are just a few of the fine weeds the Dutch have cultivated, all acclimatised Californian varieties. They are typical of the Californian brands in that they are very green even when dried and are very aromatic and potent. These seeds have no individual particular features though they are usually larger and more marbled than regular seeds due to them being of an extensively cultivated stock.

In Holland they are usually grown 'organically' in soil, or 'hydroponically', in a fertilised, oxygenated water solution/soil-less compost.

In the ideal environment these 'bud' or 'flower' are ready to harvest 45-60 days after the plant has been put into the flowering cycle (more bout that later) or 50-65 days after planting. And, as they are also '*Indica's*' or '*Indica*' mixes, they are shorter in height than most other varieties, and when it comes to buzz, they are the boom anyway.

The obvious choices when choosing a variety, may be to go for the glamorous names, check dis! '*Shiva Shanti*' and '*Hindu Kush*'. And how bout...? '*White Widow*', '*El Nino*', '*Silver Haze*'.

Nough more! But it's all glamour. These plants are really indoor plants. And when I say 'indoor' I mean the whole thing; specialist lights and professional growing equipment and tings.

But if you're growing on a balcony or in the window or in the window or some place like that and you're depending on the sun, those plants that I've just mentioned above usually wouldn't flower in time and would die before they finished flowering (due to frost, lack of light and tings).

You'd have to wait till Christmas till it was ready!

If that's the case though, it would make more sense to eschew (posh!) ... eschew the exotic names in the name of... errr... *word association*, and go for the 'Early's'. 'Early's' are Plants that begin flowering in the middle of the summer, as opposed to the middle of autumn, and is finished flowering and is ready to smoke or whatever before the Autumn has ended, even in the notably unsociable British climate. These varieties are usually prefixed by the word 'Early'. Such as *'Early Pearl'* and *'Early Girl'*.

Early flowerer's are wicked, but are not short plants being usually *'Sativa'* based with a touch of *'Ruderalis'*, but they can have a good yield.... You'll be sorted.

(2) GERMINATION (BASICS)

Watch *ya!* To germinate these seeds, do it as you would most other seeds. Put the mature brown seeds (discard white and green seeds because dem sorrft) in a dish or saucer and cover with absorbent tissue paper, dampen with water and put in a warm dark place, such as a hot water tank cupboard or somewhere like dat.

Remember to always keep the tissue paper damp, and after a few days the seeds should start to split and the rootlet should be starting to poke its lovely head through. But don't be impatient, wait another day or so, or until the rootlet is about 2mm long; it is now ready to be put into soil.

It doesn't matter when you plant, if you plant in the winter they will grow a bit slower in that there are shorter days and less light, due to the Sun moving through the sky on a lower axis. Phew.....

But grow they will, and come spring they have a massive corpasetic head start on the spring seedlings.

My solution is to grow plants at all times of the year, guaranteeing a crop at all times.

(3) POTS (BASICS)

Listen rude boy, a good advice me a give yuh now. What we need first is a bag of soil and say... fifty tiny pots, or a seedling tray with individual cells, covered. Heated or not heated. Transplant on into larger pots, the bigger the better, because a plant can only grow as much as the roots allow. And also... *'Hear some plant psychology now'*; if the pot is too small, the plant is more likely to grow into a male plant, this is because, if the roots are allowed to reach to the bottom of the pots too quickly, the pots aren't very deep. The plant checks that... and probably thinks;

"This isn't the sort of earth I want my seeds to grow up in! This soil isn't deep enough! I have the power to change my sex ... (yes they have!) ... and I'm going to be male!" (They have three sexes, male, female and hermaphrodite* all on separate plants)

Anyway!! Allow the pots to have good drainage, don't pack the soil at all, then....... Bam!!! You are part of the magic that allows plants to grow, this is so simple that it really is magic.

(4) SOILS AND FERTILISERS.
(BASICS)

*A*llrite *Ruffneck!* Try to use the best soils and
fertilisers that you can get, use shop soils such
as the soils they sell in Gro-bags or peat based soils,
these are safe as they're rich soils and also free from
any diseases or fungi. I'd say that one of... in fact,
the most valuable things on the planet are humus,
natural composts and soil.

Organic fertilisers are the best, such as horse
manure, and pigeon shit or any flying animal dung,
(collectively known as Guano) But failing to get
them I use a fertiliser such as a shop one for house
plants (nitrogen based) or any general all-purpose
plant food soluble in water. The thing with
fertilisers in general though is that they are too
strong and can easily make the plant 'O'd'. Damage
the plants like a weed-killer. Plants have a
saturation point in regards to nutrients, they don't
store the surplus fertiliser like body fat, they usually
have had no need to, the problem of a too rich soil
being an alien concept in their evolution. If the soil
content suddenly changed and got too rich in one or
another particular element, the existing plants

would die and make way for plants with particular likings and lackings for those same elements. As we all know, 'Weeds' (Wild plants and flowers) need less fertiliser than 'Cultivars' (Garden plants) In fact weeds need hardly any nutrients at all, and if you give them a little they'll take over, but use too much and they'll die, so use only half the recommended amount of fertiliser they tell you to.

Soils must never be allowed to completely dry out, but too much water can lead to stem rot, and in severe cases root rot. But still, do bear in mind that large plants need vast amounts of water so do not been afraid to water.

Some soils are too acid (acieed!!!) or too Alkaline, but this does not usually affect such an opportunistic weed as this one which seems to thrive in almost any conditions, but in extremer cases it makes the plants weaker and spindly, but usually this is nothing that a bit of good plant food won't deal with. ''Yuh know, sort out, and ting and ting.

(5)PLANT BIOLOGY (BASICS)

Yow my lion! Basically.... 'Weed' is a weed and it will grow in any soil, even impoverished soil (but not as well) If it was grown outside in the same way as say... Stinging nettles (*'Urtica Dioca'*) ''Yuh si di Latin deh!'' It would reach maturity and have optimum growth in the same way as the nettle, and in the same way, is an opportunist, which means it will grow anywhere and in almost any condition, and flourish it will, so a Council flat is more than the ideal place to grow it in.

A plant gets its sustenance from two sources, light through its leaves, and from the soil through it's roots. When solar radiation (light and heat) strikes the surface of the leaves, it causes the surface of the leaves to sweat, and this evaporation in turn is what draws the water up the stem of the plant in order to cool it down and therefore keep the temperature regulated throughout the plant. This is called 'Osmosis', and it is the reason why a plant which has more leaves will always grow faster than a plant with fewer leaves.

Remember leaves are only an extension of the roots; kind of solar panels whose purpose is to get the plants big enough so that they mature and pollinate, or are pollinated in order to perpetuate the species, for like everything alive, it wants to live and will always try to hang on to life, if not for itself, for its seeds.

'Weed' plants are split into two groups. By variety; *'Sativa'*, *'Indica'* and *'Ruderalis'*, and by sex; Male and Female.

To know which is *'Sativa'*, which is *'Indica'* and which is *'Ruderalis'* is not very important to you or I at the moment, but basically, *'Sativas'* are tall slim leafed hot climate plants more used to harsher sunlight than the other types.

'Indicas' are more temperate and have wider leaves and are shorter and squatter than *'Sativas'*,

The ... errr... flowers ... 'Buds' are the largest of the three varieties and are the most resinous.

Both *'Sativas'* and *'Indicas'* are 'Photo-periodic'; responsive to the amount of darkness/light they receive in regards to their flowering cycle.

'Ruderalis's' are rarely cultivated and are very small plants. They are found mostly in the Northern Hemisphere in the colder climates, and are not Photo-periodic. Instead they flower when reaching a certain size or age. Usually they start flowering at the fifth, sixth, seventh, eighth 'inter-nodes', [sets

of leaves], depending on the parent. They start quite young though, as they are aclimitised to be in the unmercifully short northern summers near the Arctic circle and beyond.

Out of the three, *'Indicas'* yield the most and are the most potent, as well as having a shorter growing and flowering season than the *'Sativas'*, but as for the difference between males and females? These differences are more than important, as only the female plants carry the potency in the buds for which these plants are famed, and only the females are pollinated and can therefore seed.

Unlike most other plants, weed plants do not commonly carry both sexes of flower on the same plant (*'Monoecious'*. They have separate plants for each gender, (*'Dioecious'*), and then there is also the *'Monoecious Hermaphrodites'* type of weed.

'Allrite, just cool. What I suppose I mean is that the females are the plants that you can smoke and get buzzed. Sheesh! Alright now, yuh satisfied? I wrote it, see!' (the tings yuh have fe do nowadays to keep di woman cool) 'Yes dear, I'll be there in a minute.

F

M

M opened

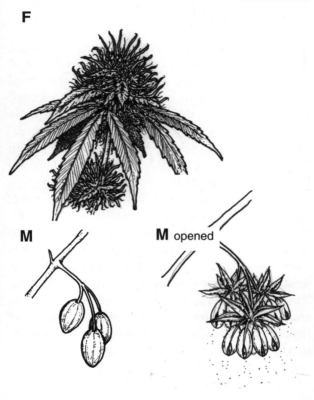

(6) TREATMENT & CARE.

I have gone through the 'care 'from seeds to plants, and now we get to the real important bit. Most of you who are reading this have probably tried growing weed before but have had little success. This is basically through greed. What usually happens is that as soon as your plants grew to a reasonable size, you pick the leaves off, starting with the main leaves (the big 3-5-7-9-11 pronged leaves) ('Palmate' - as in hand).

This is one of the biggest mistakes you can make. It needs every leaf it can get. Ideally you shouldn't pick off any leaves to smoke, but if you have to do that, do not take off the biggest leaves, it needs them. If anything, take off the most succulent immature top buds and leaves, for if it has big leaves it will continue to grow replacement buds and leaves. However it cannot grow the replacement main leaves which is what it needs for maximum surface area to enable the process of maximum 'Osmosis' and 'Photosynthesis'.

I know it sounds simple, but follow this and your plants will attain maximum growth in the shortest possible time.

If you grow enough plants you and them will not

notice this pruning. But why do it? ... Why bother? Have some patience! Wait for the flowers to mature; it's ten times better.

So I cannot stress this too much; **if you take off the main leaves your plant will not mature readily and will only be a 'leafy tea' plant.**

Normally, when a plant is ready to be harvested the main leaves fall off, the leaves having given all its energy back to the plant, ... leaving only the buds (flowers) and small leaves.

The leaves are also a buffer from a lot of toxins or harmful substances as they accumulate in the leaves, allowing the plants to shed them when necessary.

So leaving them on has even more importance than what is usually apparent.

(7) PESTS & PROBLEMS:

blackfly, greenfly, stemrot, overfertilising.

Boom *bye bye in a aphid head!! Fungi and parasite dem ha fi dead'*. In the council flat environment, there are not a lot of things that can go wrong with your weed plants, but there are some.

Blackfly and Greenfly are more of a pest than a problem, and are easily remedied by most popular brands of insecticide.

However, if you are of a more organic constitution, you can make effective insecticides from common household products such as Chilli pepper powder made up in a weak solution in water (never use salt ever) or use tobacco soaked water.

(Incidentally I have theory.... When Sir Walter Raleigh visited South America the native people dem originally give him Ganja to smoke, but when he was ready to go back to England, it seems he went to some people that he shouldn't have and *he got ripped off* ... They sold him a 'formula' HA HA! They sold him *tobacco*!! Or they sold the dealers who went after him tobacco. Could this be the proper history of tobacco? Could tobacco be just another insecticide?

'You see rude bwoy, we know dem tings deh.'

Anyway.... *Tobacco*! The resulting liquids are then sprayed over the affected plant.

'But you see stem rot!.... hmmuh!'

This problem is caused by too wet a topsoil. It is compounded when decaying plant material is left in the pot, such as wet green leaves. When damped with water, they begin to decay, promoting fungal growth and breaking down into an acidic solution. (Y'know? It's like the ponds in autumn with a rainbow film on top of it that looks like someone's poured some oil in it, but in fact it is the acid from the decaying Autumn leaves breaking down in solution).

For this I take *no* risks! I use a shop bought fungicide. Fresh leaves and dead leaves are useless as a fertiliser anyway (why do you think people make compost heaps anyway?!) well that's the reason.

You can help to prevent it by watering the dish at the bottom of the pot, but not watering it too much.

You can tell when a plant is over-watered in that the lowest leaves turn prematurely yellow and fall off, and the whole plant takes on a wanner lighter complexion.

Another reason for the young leaves yellowing if it isn't over-watered, especially when they're shrivelling, will probably be a Sulphur deficiency. Give it a little food. Not a lot, just a little.

If you want to get technical you can check out a Sulphur preparation. If it's turning yellow around the veins of the leaves, that sounds like a Magnesium deficiency. They sell magnesium-sulphur compounds on the market. Fertiliser in small amounts is just as good.

Iron deficiency is similar except that the yellowing is more widespread and the leaves sag. I'd go for 'Guano', a natural fertiliser. A little expensive maybe, but it works.

If your leaves have a patchwork type of effect, a mosaic type of pattern on the leaves and they are brittle, this would indicate the presence of harmful fungi in the soil.

If the soil is packed in the pot without worms to turn the soil, the soil will get compacted at the bottom of the pots, this cuts down the oxygen, and combined with a little heat, forms its own Fungi colony.

A 3 parts soil, one part vermiculite soil mixture helps to stop this problem, the vermiculite aerating the soil in place of worms. Not perfect, but adequate.

Under-watering is easily remedied. I will not design to insult your intelligence by telling you the solution to this.

If your plant is sagging, though still a healthy green, it is usually suffering from under-watering. Your plants (especially in the later stages of their lives), may need vast amounts of water and you will need to water them nearly everyday.

Try to water them through the dishes at the bottom of the pots, unless your fertiliser has to be put onto the topsoil. If so, then water in small stages until a small amount of water is left in the base dish.

When your plant has had enough water and it's looking like those big sun leaves, the oldest leaves, are too dark and /or they start curling; this indicates a Phosphorus deficiency. 'Guano', Seaweed 'ferts' or even a regular fertiliser, with Phosphate sorts this.

When a plant is under-fertilised it is basically undernourished so it looks weak and spindly etc. Again this is easily remedied.

What is more of a problem is over fertilising. This shows itself on the leaves as a burnt leaf effect, especially on the new buds and leaves, stunting them and almost seeming to reverse plant maturity.

It causes new leaves to turn into themselves and wither to lesser or greater degrees, sometimes taking on an unhealthy silvery sheen. Confusingly the symptoms can also look like an undernourished plant!

I usually do what I call 'flush them out' to cure them, which is basically excessively over-water to the max! Flood! And then drain off the excess water a few times if necessary. I then discard the water and hope, because there's not much that you can do to help a plant in this condition, but I think it's worth a try.

Another reason why a plant may be sagging is that it has not had enough light. Alright, I know this may sound obvious but as we know weed trees need a lot of light.... or do they?

Well contrary to a lot of peoples thinking, they don't need as much light as what you would think. They need open light, not reflected light. Water, and a little bit of light and a lot of air is more important than a lot of light and not enough water and air. A 50 watt fluorescent tube is enough for a medium sized plant and can easily start off your seedlings and cuttings and make your small plants flourish.

Of course if you want to get hardcore on it and stuff, you could go for bigger lights and the whole set-up. But that's a completely different book.

You can give a plant15, 18 or even 24 hours of light a day. Although even plants need sleep, 24 hours of light a day over too long a period may, and eventually will harm them.

Listen... 'Photosynthesis' is the sun powered manufacture of sugers within the green parts of a plant, which requires water and carbon dioxide while producing oxygen. This happens only when there is light. When it's dark the reverse happens and then it produces carbon dioxide. If it doesn't complete the cycle for too long, it can die of exhaustion, or it can have its immune system compromised leaving it open for predation and/or disease.

When you want your plants to flower or 'bud' this is attainable by shortening the amount of light it receives to 11-12 hrs. This tricks it into believing that it is now the end of the season! So it gets ready to 'pollinate' or be 'pollinated', in other words 'Bud' or 'flower'.

This only works on plants with a root system.

Depending on the strength of the lights and the nature of plants, results can be seen within two weeks or earlier.

I was going to go on about lights and growing seasons at the Equator, how it relates to Europe and more importantly how it relates to your council flat, but I'm not convinced of it's relevancy, as I might only succeed in getting your hopes up, or worse still, I might sound like I'm soft.

(8) MATURITY (BASICS)
SEXING AND SEPARATION

Yow Star, dis isn't no kind of porno business, or no celibacy thing, this is plants, so hold tight. The males always reach maturity first, approximately one or two weeks before the females. The male flowers are light green and are about 3mm long, they are slightly reminiscent of snowdrops and are useless for anything except pollinating the females.

No, there is no secret buzz lurking in the flowers of the male plant, which is best being disposed of in any way you see fit.

'Dem taste bad yuh si! Yeuk!'

Anyway, it is at this time that sexing takes place. Sexing means to separate the female and male plants so that pollination does not occur.

Pollination in this plant is by wind and rarely by insects. This is evidenced by the downward drooping flowers on the taller males, dropping copious amounts of pollen on the shorter females, and by the receptive stickiness of the female flowers, so insects are discouraged.

If both sexes are together, the very action of

opening and closing the door will cause wind pollination within that room, and one grain of pollen will in turn become one seed. (I bet you never knew that).

Separate them as soon as you can spot the males flowering. Then you can concentrate on controlling the pollination of individual plants by means of transferring the pollen manually.

You can 'pseudo' change the sex of your male plants by removing the male flowerheads as soon as they appear and after about a month they seem to change sex!

This is because all male plants will actually produce a few female flower heads at the onset of the 'late stage' of its maturity (and vice versa). Just in case it doesn't pollinate other plants, it can keep its line alive by either pollinating itself, or by being pollinated by another plant.

The action of removing the male flowers can cause the female flowers to be stimulated and grow, but this is not guaranteed and usually takes about six weeks or longer (waste of time, and not worth it).

The female plant is usually shorter and sturdier, but that is also not guaranteed. The female flowers are not easily recognisable as they do not have the normal shape and colouring expected of flowers in that they are indistinct and have no strong colouring. They are green and appear to be just a mass profusion of leaf buds interspersed with light coloured or white plant hairs turning brown over time. 3-10mm long. The whole of which is aromatic and sticky with resin, more so as it nears maturity.

Incidentally, these are the only parts of the plants worth smoking. These are 'Heads'. The rest of the plant, the stems, stalks, leaves, seeds and roots are all useless for smoking as is the complete male plant.

The reason why the female flowers are sticky is that it gives it an advantage in the wind pollinated world, in that a grain of pollen, once that it has been caught, it stays caught.

The advantage to us is that if it is not pollinated, to give itself more of a chance, it will increase it's bud size and secrete more resin, thus increasing its chances of catching pollen, and if it is not pollinated at all, all the energy it would have used in producing seeds, it now uses to make a succulent sticky seed-less pungent bud; *'Sensimillia'*. Although it's always good to have a tree which you can pollinate, ensuring a more acclimatised crop for next year.

But be warned, once you get the tree to yield its seed, it will have completed it's life cycle and the plant will die, so you will not get a second or third crop from your tree.

Yes! With careful cropping you will easily get two crops, and maybe three crops, as long as you follow the general rule and only crop the buds and not the leaves.

After cropping, put the plants back into 13 or more hours of light a day, this takes it out of flowering mode, back into the vegetative mode, or regenerative mode. After about three weeks it is ready to go back to the flowering mode, over twelve hours of darkness.

Another wonderful trick used by weed seed breeders is to leave the female tree unpollinated until it produces male flowers to pollinate itself with mostly female pollen. This can be collected and used on other female plants, the resulting seeds will nearly always be female. Upwards of 70/30 as opposed to the 40/60 of normal crossed pollination.

(9)CURING (basics) and mis(myth)conceptions

Basically curing is a myth, you could not take a male plant and by a special process cure it and make it as strong as the female plant, and so it is with the leaves and stalks. You couldn't cure these and make them as strong as the buds. Laying it on the damp soil in a humid atmosphere. (fungi weather, watch out!!) ....will take away the greenness, but it will not make it any stronger, even hanging it upside down by the roots only helps it minimally. This is because after the tree has been cut down or uprooted, there is no more resin being produced, so it will not get any stronger, only drier.

Incidentally, micro-waving, grilling and other ways of force drying seems to make it weaker, and definitely greener, so do try to dry it naturally and slowly. This could be on the floor of your living room, then wait until it's nearly dry, pick up and pack loosely together and keep in a dry ventilated place until it is ready to be smoked,

.....then...

AAAH! ....FRESH WEED!!..

(10) DISGUISES.

(how to get away with it)

Fix up and look sharp like Dizzee! This is a very important issue in this time as we all know the legalities, or should I say the illegalities of growing your 'own'. It seems that this is such an appealing bush, that many people are seeking to find out where it is and take it for themselves.

Police aren't bothering with the helicopters again like they used to, as they've finally realised that it's stupid to spend thousands of pounds trying to stop something that is so prevalent and common place (etc).

But then there's the neighbours who feel like doing a good turn for the police by telling them about your plants (*dodgy!!*)

And of course there's the people who spotted it by its shape or some other reason, and are probably right now waiting for you to go out so that they can break into your home and steal all your plants.

Yes we do have a lot of problems. So disguises are good, plastic fruit, cherries, good. Tomatoes good. Cloth or paper flowers? It's all good.

But be careful, be safe! Use a condom! Hide your plants from prying eyes! Don't run with a tooth-brush in your mouth. Don't wear one of your plants as a hat.

Update 2004:

Since I wrote the first edition of this back in 1988 the political situation regarding weed in Council flats have changed.

If you get busted now dealing or growing weed in your Council flat and the Council finds out, the Council can and may kick you out, effectively turning your Council Flat Paradise into a homeless nightmare. Chhuuh!

(11) CUTTINGS. (basics)

Cuttings are simply obtained by cutting off one of the small succulent branches, (5cms and up) discard the lower leaves and place the cutting in a small container such as a glass or a used and cleaned Yoghurt pot, fill with water and leave in a warm place with indirect light. (sunshine is best, but fluorescents are also great) you can add a small amount of rooting powder to the water if you think it needs a little help, but do not change the water till you can see roots. It will live and grow roots as is its nature, and when the roots are as big as the foliage on the cutting itself, then that is the time to plant on into soil. ...

But all that is just to show you how easy it is. The best way is to take the cutting as before and coat the lower half of the stem with rooting powder and just stick it in sodden soil or compost, while keeping the temperature of it around 25 degrees, nice and humid. What's even better is one of those cuttings trays, covered. Some of them's even heated.

If you want to grow them hydroponically you'd have to root them in rock-wool or some other inert medium.

(A little tip... If you're using soil, break them out

of the cuttings tray like how the native Americans used to break in horses, ... in water. It is less damaging and stressful to the roots as it is not supporting its own weight.

' But enough Horseplay...'

Cuttings are actually, scientifically, 'Clones', but they don't need a womb or a test tube or any of those things. It happens in the wild all the time in the plant kingdom, some plant's natural way of reproduction is by cloning. The humble Potato for instance; clone.

An advantage of cloning is choosing the mother plant for its vigour potency and sex. This way you will only get vigorous potent plants of the sex of your choice, and if you can manage the subtle art of grafting.... (you would find out why the slang term 'grafting' is used to describe very hard and tedious work) .... grafting one cutting onto another plant you would have a plant that is impossible to seed.

Yes! No seeds, even if it was covered in pollen. You see Nature has a great law in that, only a plant that has grown from its own root system can in turn yield seeds. (I'd say that we are exploiting a loop-hole here bad bwoy) Sounds strange yeah!! So where do you think we get seedless grapes from then????? By the way it isn't possible to graft weed onto hops and vice versa, they're not really in the same family, that's a myth, a 'Linnaen' myth. Check it out!

Weed is a kind of shrub kind of plant, while Hops are Vines! No relation at all, genetically or otherwise, except in the Linnaen sense. Linnaeus (the father of taxonomy) classified plants into families, determined by the amount of, and by the length of its Stamens. This method also puts 'Cacti' and 'Cherry' in the same family!

(12) HYDROPONICS.(basics)

Check dis star!! Some heavy business now! Hydroponics is a way of growing plants without soil. Instead of soil a covered grid or some net-like structure is braced over a nutrient rich moving water solution. (an aquarium 'bubbler' is perfect for this) the roots of the cuttings hang in the oxygen and nutrient rich water through and supported by the 'net' immersed in liquid as it was when it was sitting in a glass or a yoghurt pot.

It's a bit more complicated than growing it on a windowsill though, and actually takes quite a lot of work and expense to set up, as well as having to acquire a knowledge of chemicals, chemical densities, and concentration levels, pH's, as well as plumbing.

13) FLOWERING basics

Honour to all the crews! Respect! Anklespect! *Footspect in a every aspect!* Everybody keeps on going about light, and though light is important, in fact *vital* for a weed plant when it's growing, what is even more important when you want it to flower is darkness. Yes darkness! The reason is ... and here I'm going to get *scientifical* and ting....

If you left the weed to it's own devices, it would flower at the end of the season in about October when the darkness has increased to about twelve hours and more.

You see, weed is a night flowering plant as are many other plants such as.... *'Chrysanthemums'*, *'Michaelmas Daisies'*, *'Autumn Crocus'* and many more.

This fact is commonly known and put to use by commercial growers who would never wait a year when there's money to be made all year round. Especially when flowering is easily attained anytime by just sticking them in a completely dark room or turning off the lights for twelve hours,

Bear in mind: The energy a plant gathers by day in the form of light is the energy which it uses to create its flowers at night, the optimum being between 10.5-12 hours light a day.

Now we get to the scientific part.

'You thought that was it, init!? Well *listen*!'

When a night flowering plant has been kept in uninterrupted darkness for about 11 hours the plant begins to produce a flowering hormone; *'Florigen'**. This stimulates new leaf growth into flower.

At twelve hours of uninterrupted darkness, the *'Florigen'* is fully active, and at twelve and a half hours it is positively rampant, but more than thirteen, and the hormone is on the wane having spent the daylight energy in its production.

Resin also, is only produced at night. What we smell in the daytime from it is evaporation, so the best time to crop the plants is at the end of its night cycle.

*Florigen is extremely light sensitive, so light sensitive that it cannot be seen in any of the light frequencies, as light destroys it. So to attain flowering, the rule of uninterrupted darkness is to be followed. (Photoperiodism; the response of plants, such as flowering and fruiting to relative lengths of light and darkness) This technique will even work on your cuttings, so you can see, or should I say... taste, what kind of herb you've got.

14) SOIL (not just dirt)

Millions of years before man evolved plants had already solved all sorts of problems from Plumbing to Structural Engineering.

They had already mastered Hydrodynamics and Aerodynamics (while dabbling in a bit of Thermodynamics on the side) and had already developed a multitude of various gadgets to ensure their survival.

But we Human Beings are in a rush and also in a panic as the population increases and threatens to outstrip the world's ability to support us. And in our panic we fail to realise what our sudden and inept action inevitably does to the delicate balance of the planet.

Our presumptuousness leads us to doubt the intimate relationship between plants and soil, or is it our disconnection from the soil that makes us doubt it? (whatever).

And, instead of us regarding soil as life giving, we tend to think of it more as 'Dirt', harbouring diseases and harmful organisms, and that 'clean' mediums such as 'Rockwool' and expanded clay pebbles are better.

It would be reasonable to compare soil to an

extremely complex and technical chemical laboratory, in which a large number of reactions involving almost every known element takes place.

Certain reactions are comparatively simple of course and well understood, but most of them are extremely complicated and not understood by science at all.

Some of the elements most important to plant nutrition include, Phosphorus, Sulphur, Nitrogen, Calcium, Iron and Magnesium.

Plants also need small but significant quantities of such elements as Boron, Copper, manganese and Zinc in order for them to flourish. Alright! this is just my speculation here, I know it might sound radical. But maybe plants need *all* the elements that are in soil in lesser and greater amounts, it may be that they *all* do some small but significant thing. It's a wild guess I know, but maybe... just maybe ...

I mean, well... I 'puff' because it's natural and free of additives and tings (presumably), untouched by the system (apparently).

That's about the whole gist of my argument, (..er.. actually) which up to now has stood me in good stead (incidentally!)

But recently I've been mostly smoking 'Skunk'

weed types, and I've noticed that quite a lot of people think it's some kind of 'genetically engineered' Class A designer drug, it's 'B' going to C going to...? And another ting ... 'Skunk' has been *selectively bred* as opposed to 'genetically modified'.

And because it's so strong, some people mistrust it, even preferring to smoke low grade bush or even crap repressed Euro-soap hash! While some are just opposed to 'Skunk' on political grounds. Well this isn't the first time that this has happened. It's already happened and is happening in Holland where they prefer their stuff a bit more organic. Let's face it. Holland run tings'. They lead, we follow.

Not surprising really, it's legal over there. They've already got the best Greenhouse and indoor growing technology in the world, tested over time and used or rejected. (.... wonder where the rejects go?)

Their backlash started several years ago in the Coffee Shops, away from the view of the customers. The Cafe weed Sellers can afford to be fussy and buy the best, and that's why they pay more for the soil grown stuff than for the 'Hydro'.

'How can they tell?' You think.

Well they taste it. They say they can taste the rock-wool, and especially the chemicals. (and when they tell you the names of the feeds that you've used, you tend to believe) And it's harder to sell gear that hasn't been 'flushed'.

'Flushing' is when you don't feed the plants any nutrients at all for the last couple of weeks. In the 'Hydro' systems this means replacing and circulating pure water through the system and discarding the old nutrient filled water. This doesn't harm the plants at all, they have more than enough nutrients stored as cellulose's and sugars in their systems to keep them healthy for even longer periods.

Also looked at is the density and cohesiveness of the buds, or in other words, is it going to flake off like dandruff leaving lots of un-saleable dust and chaff at the bottom of the bag? ....All right! We yield to market forces, and let's face it, in Holland the Cafe sellers dictate the terms, both to the punters and the growers, and they're not interested in how fancily it's grown, it could be some Interstellar irradiated aero-hydroponic null gravity grown cyberclonic weed or something. They taste.

They like. They buy. It's simple really.... In Britain it's a lot different though. No one dictates the terms (Good!) but there is no kind of quality control at all. (not good) People take what they can get.

'Is it green? Has it got the smell? Is it Skunk? .... Yes? ... I'll ave some a that then.' Is usually the way that it's bought and sold in the U.K. ... No more questions need to be asked really. This is the U.K. It'll sell! ... What other questions?

'But it's all chemical hydroponic weed isn't it?' is the general consensus and opinion of 'Skunk'; that it's an unnatural weed of human design.

For while the rest of the world seems to be embracing the green revolution. Only the scientists and their other parallels in horticulture and business, the weed growers, are eager to embrace technology in the continuing search for quantity over quality. While not thinking or even considering what the health effects on us may be.

'But what about the trees that grows by the rivers of waters?' I hear my Rastafarian grower friend quote-eth, implying something hydroponic. *'No other trees are as strong as the trees that grow by the rivers of waters!'*

'That's true, but they do get sufficient water all the

time 'Dread'.

They never or rarely lack for water like most of the other non water dwelling trees, and even then they don't have all their roots in the water.

Plants evolved in water and then chose to leave it for their own betterment. If it was an advantage to them to stay in water they probably would have, ...I'm not being anti hydroponics, I'm just supporting soil.

'Aah! But you get more yield using Hydro! Don't you?' My friend from the Wirral presumes doubtfully.

I answer in kind.

'Kind of.... You do and you don't. It's debatable if you get bigger sized buds or not, in weight and size, and when they're bigger they're not as dense.'

'But if you do the Hydro right.....' Suggests another grower.

'Oh yeah Smiffy! If you do it right!' I mock. 'You only get about one out of every three of your grows right. ...If that!

There's always problems with plumbing and too much feed, too little of this or that nutrient or chemicals, P.H messing up, Pythium etc etc..... I know that a Hydro set-up looks beautiful in it's own way. It's modern technology, science, smooth surfaces, no bits of soil everywhere, clean and pure, shiny, standardised. *Sieg heil! Sieg heil!*

Have we developed an obsession with standardisation and conformism?

..... Yes I suppose we have already, it's called 'Fashion'. And the lengths that we'll go to, to feel fashionable.... Even if it doesn't work.

'THC' in plants is made up of many different compounds, what their devices are and how their combinations and concentrations are made up is still a mystery to us.

And though plants are able to change one element to another at the atomic level in a undetermined form of cold fusion or something, from 'fixing' (gathering) selected elements from their environments and changing them if necessary, they do need more than the basic elements that we are able to formulate as feeds for them.

As I said before, in nature, plants take up a lot of things they don't use, or what researchers haven't yet found a reason for them being there.

Iodine for example, plants absorb, but as far as we know, don't use, but we do! We need it for our thyroid glands amongst other things.

Apparently if you're a Vegan and you lived totally off hydroponically produced food, you'd end up with a whole load of mineral deficiencies. So maybe the herb could be getting deficient in.......'

'But do you get a better Yield? Weight wise, from the hydro?' The voice of the true commercial grower interrupts, going straight to the point again.

'Per crop you mean? In a perfect environment?' I answer, 'well there's no proof that you do ... unless you believe the manufacturers claims, though it could be a bit one sided as 'Nature' hasn't got the same marketing skills.

You'd have to go to Holland and listen to their superior experience to answer that, and they say 'No, there really isn't any difference weight wise. It mostly depends on care.'

'But it's easier to set up, easier to use, and less messy overall isn't it?'

'Well I suppose it's less messy....' I pause with comic timing .... 'though the weight of the water is quite heavy, and that puts a lot of pressure on the seals which can leak.'

And of course maybe we should limit our dumping of nutrients into the ecosy stem. Already the tipping of used engine oils by DIY mechanics into the drains and sewers is becoming a major source of world oil pollution.

And, as the popularity of Hydroponics spreads, maybe we should be trying to look at the metaphorical horizon of it all and notice that there's got to be a significant risk of potential damage to the environment from carelessly disposed runoff, dumped solutions and other waste media.

As for it being easier to set up and use, I suppose it only takes a few days to sort out, with getting everything right, sorting out the solutions and the pH's, the concentrations and the conductivity of the feeds, water temperature, the pipes, the seals, connections, the trays, pots, bubbler's, pumps, timers and the rest of the electric's and a few more things that I've probably forgotten.....

Oh yeah! The plants! You see what I mean? The thinking sometimes goes; 'That if you're looking after the system, the system will look after the plants'.

... So you spend all the time looking after the system, learning how to measure things even more accurately. And all the while you're not looking after the plants anymore.

.... And if it goes wrong! You blame yourself ...

chiding yourself that you didn't do it right ... but sometimes it's the system that's wrong.

All right I'll get to the point. The point for some people is 'Money', 'Dollars', 'Wonga', 'Moola'.

You don't want to fail, you can't *afford* to fail! You're not an expert, even though you may believe you are, and compared to some you may be, but lets get real, anything can happen, and sometimes does.

A seal goes and a roof is flooded, it may delay the program or stop it altogether. Or you've overfed your plants (public enemy problem no.1!) that may also delay the program or stop it altogether. Too acid or too alkaloid? Delay or finito. Basically there is nothing to protect the roots from your mistakes.

That's why in Holland when it comes to weed, 'Hydroponics' is usually for the hobby grower who wants to grow five or ten plants.

When it's time to get serious though, a system with a well chosen buffering medium is a wiser alternative.

For example, plants potted in compost, (deep pots) resting on capillary matting or soil bed, watered and fed, with always less fertiliser than the recommended amount, by 'flood and leave it alone' to allow the pots to soak up the excess. Sounds simple, but it works, everytime.

Capillary matting is very important. Under no circumstances must you use *white capillary matting.

There is no such thing as white capillary matting, because it would go green with Algae and harm the roots, and roots need darkness to be able to function efficiently, not a net curtain.

(*especially 'Frostguard') 'Frostguard' is the thin white nylon fibre type sheets (about 1mm thick) that are traditionally used to protect your garden plants from frost. It is not capillary matting though it is sometimes sold as such.

Capillary matting is green or black or other dark colours and is 3mm thick and upwards.

Another alternative is to rest your pots on a soil bed. Pots are quite important as an aid to pest control in all systems if the need to individualise particular plants arises.

'Perlite' mixed with soil as a growing medium is very good as it is organic, being a volcanic substance. But because of the harshness and intensity of the lighting needed to grow Weed, it is not ideal as it is white, and so in the presence of water, light and heat it also goes green.

An alternative mix is 'Vermiculite'. Both mediums not only retain water but also aerate the soil in the absence of worms, which are not encouraged.

It's hard to take on new ideas, and it's even harder to take on new old ideas. Experimenting is part of our nature, and we've got to try it all. So to sign off I'll give you an easy experiment in three parts that won't cost you anything.

1) Go into your local garden store DIY or super-market with its poor to average lighting and look at their soil grown plants.

2) Go into a Hydroponics stockist with its great lighting and have a look at their hydroponically grown plants.

3) Compare.

(14b) SOILS.(again)
Purple weed?

What normally happens with soil in an outdoor environment is that foliage on plants die and fall to the ground, they are then consumed and recycled by the action of the elements, (weather, temperature, organic chemical reactions) they are exploited by fungi and insects and broken down to form more soil and nutrients which will keep the soil balanced and fertilised for the next year. But in a potted plant, all the leaves that fall onto the soil must be removed. So fertiliser is vital as the leaves have not yet broken down into a form that the plant can use.

A few of the varieties which are sometimes grown have strange coloured foliage. In some varieties it is natural for the plant to come fully loaded with orange leaves and buds of various different hues. These types are natural and pleasant. The leaves and buds of over mature plants can also turn purple as so can plants that are grown under lighting that is insufficient in certain spectrums, it may also indicate an imbalance in the feed, and also an indication of a pest such as the Fungus root mould fly, whose larvae eats roots.

Soils also come in all different colours. Some soils are red are have a reddish tint to it which can indicate the presence of Aluminium. Weeds that are grown in these soils can have a reddish blush.. (blush?) ..to them.

When copper is present, the foliage tends to take on an even darker colouring. Some people plough these elements directly into the soil, on their voyage of discovery, to get the desired effects with.... less than average results.

But are you sure? Do you really want to smoke metals? I don't. it doesn't make it any stronger or vibesier.

Personally I definitely prefer a green plant anytime, a nice healthy green balanced pure green plant, for...like my water, I like my weed pure as well.....

Well that's it People... Hold tight , cah wha? This is the author signing off wid de detrimental poisonous dettol maxifillated turbo fuel grandfather X-ray pen biznizz. Just cool.....

Happy growing!!!!!

NOTES

NOTES